THE DOLLARS DEMISE

By:Dashaun Wade-Bouie

THE DOLLARS DEMISE

THE DOLLARS DEMISE

Disclaimer Notice

The information contained in this book is for general informational purposes only. While we strive to provide accurate and up-to-date information, we make no representations or warranties of any kind, express or implied, about the completeness, accuracy, reliability, suitability, or availability with respect to the book or the information, products, services, or related graphics contained within for any purpose. Any reliance you place on such information is therefore strictly at your own risk.

Legal Notice

Chapter 1

What is a US dollar crash

The US dollar is the world's primary reserve currency, meaning it's widely used in international trade and finance. Its stability and strength are critical to global economic stability. However, a US dollar crash can occur when the value of the dollar decreases significantly and rapidly in comparison to other currencies.A US dollar crash can be caused by a range of factors, including economic, political, and global events. Economic factors that could trigger a US dollar crash include high levels of national debt, inflation, or a decrease in foreign investment. Political factors could include political instability, policy changes, or shifts in international relations. Global events such as natural disasters, wars, or pandemics could also lead to a US dollar crash.Historical examples of previous currency crashes provide insight into the potential impacts of a US dollar crash. From the German hyperinflation of the 1920s to the Asian financial crisis of the 1990s and the more recent Turkish currency crash of 2018, these events demonstrate the far-reaching and devastating consequences of currency instability. The German hyperinflation caused widespread economic and social unrest, while the Asian financial crisis led to financial crises and economic downturns in multiple countries. The Turkish currency crash had severe implications for the Turkish economy, with citizens facing increased living costs and a decrease in foreign investment. These examples highlight the importance of understanding the causes and implications of currency crashes and the need for preparedness in the event of a US dollar crash. Understanding the impact of a US dollar crash is essential for investors, policymakers, and individuals alike. The US dollar is the world's primary reserve currency, meaning that many countries hold it as a reserve asset and use it in international trade. A US dollar crash could trigger a significant shift in the global economy, potentially leading to a financial crisis or economic recession. For investors, a US dollar crash could mean significant losses in their portfolios, as investments denominated in US dollars would decrease in value. Policymakers would need to be prepared to manage the potential economic fallout, implementing measures to mitigate inflation, protect jobs, and stabilize the financial system. For individuals, a US dollar crash could lead to a decrease in purchasing power, making it harder to afford basic goods and services. It's crucial to understand the risks associated with a US dollar crash and be prepared for potential economic shifts. By understanding the causes and implications of a US dollar crash, individuals and organizations can take proactive measures to protect their financial well-being and mitigate potential economic disrup

Chapter 2

Causes of US dollar crash

A US dollar crash could be triggered by a range of economic factors. One potential factor is the US government's fiscal policy. The US has a large and growing national debt, and if investors lose confidence in the government's ability to pay it back, they may demand higher interest rates or sell off their US government bonds. This could lead to a rapid decline in the value of the US dollar.

Another factor is the US trade deficit. The US imports more goods and services than it exports, meaning that it needs to borrow money from other countries to pay for these imports. If foreign investors become wary of financing the US trade deficit, they may sell off US assets, leading to a decline in the value of the US dollar. Additionally, inflation can also impact the value of the US dollar. If inflation rates in the US are higher than those in other countries, the purchasing power of the US dollar decreases, making it less attractive to investors. Finally, global economic shifts could also impact the US dollar. For example, if another country becomes a more attractive destination for investors, they may sell off US assets and buy assets in that country, leading to a decline in the value of the US dollar.

A US dollar crash could be triggered by a range of economic factors. One potential factor is the US government's fiscal policy. The US has a large and growing national debt, and if investors lose confidence in the government's ability to pay it back, they may demand higher interest rates or sell off their US government bonds. This could lead to a rapid decline in the value of the US dollar. Another factor is the US trade deficit. The US imports more goods and services than it exports, meaning that it needs to borrow money from other countries to pay for these imports. If foreign investors become wary of financing the US trade deficit, they may sell off US assets, leading to a decline in the value of the US dollar. Additionally, inflation can also impact the value of the US dollar. If inflation rates in the US are higher than those in other countries, the purchasing power of the US dollar decreases, making it less attractive to investors. Finally, global economic shifts could also impact the US dollar. For example, if another country becomes a more attractive destination for investors, they may sell off US assets and buy assets in that country, leading to a decline in the value of the US dollar. Global events can have a significant impact on the value of the US dollar and potentially trigger a US dollar crash. One potential trigger could be a global economic downturn or recession. If there is a global recession, investors may become risk-averse and move their investments to safe-haven currencies, such as the Japanese yen or Swiss franc, leading to a decline in the value of the US dollar. Another potential trigger could be a significant shift in the global energy market. The US dollar is the primary currency used for trading oil, and if another currency, such as the Chinese yuan, were to become a more widely accepted currency for oil trading, this could lead to a decrease in demand for the US dollar and a decline in its value. Additionally, major geopolitical events, such as a war or a significant natural disaster, could also impact the value of the US dollar. For example, if a major natural disaster were to occur in the US, this could lead to a significant increase in government spending, potentially leading to inflation and a decrease in the value of the US dollar.

Chapter 3

Implications of a US Dollar Crash

A US dollar crash could have a significant impact on global trade and commerce. The US dollar is the world's reserve currency, meaning that it is widely used in international transactions, including trade and investment. If the value of the US dollar were to decline significantly, this could make imports into the US cost more and reduce the purchasing power of US consumers. Additionally, it could make US exports more competitive in international markets, but also it could lead to inflation and potentially hurt US companies that rely on imports or have large $ amounts of foreign debt. The impact on other countries would depend on their level of dependence on the US economy and the US dollar. For countries that have significant trade ties with the US, a US dollar crash could lead to a low demand for their goods and services, potentially leading to a decrease in their economic growth. On the other hand, countries that are less dependent on the US dollar or have diversified their economies may not be affected so much by a US dollar crash.

A US dollar crash could have a significant impact on national debt and financial stability. The US gov and many other countries have significant amounts of debt denominated in US dollars. If the value of the US dollar were to decline significantly, this could lead to an huge increase in the real value of this debt, potentially leading to a debt crisis. Additionally, a US dollar crash could lead to increased levels of inflation, which could lead to higher interest rates and a decrease in the value of bonds and other fixed-income securities. This could hurt pension funds, insurance companies, and other investors that rely on these types of investments. It could also make it more difficult for governments and companies to borrow money, potentially leading to a decrease in investment and economic growth. Furthermore, a US dollar crash could lead to financial instability in other countries, particularly those with high levels of US dollar-denominated debt. This could lead to a global financial crisis, similar to the one that occurred in 2008.Investors may also become more risk-averse and move their investments to safe-haven currencies, such as the Japanese yen or Swiss franc, leading to a decline in demand for the US dollar and a further decline in its value. Furthermore, a US dollar crash could have a significant impact on international investments, particularly in emerging markets. If the US dollar were to decline significantly, this could lead to a decline in the value of emerging market currencies and potentially hurt investors with significant holdings in those currencies.

Chapter 4

Prepairng for possible US dollar crash

Diversifying investments is crucial in minimizing the risks associated with a US dollar crash. If the US dollar were to experience a significant decline in value, it could have a negative impact on investments denominated in US dollars. To minimize this risk, investors can diversify their investments by investing in assets denominated in other currencies or assets that are not tied to the US dollar. For example, investors could consider investing in international stocks, bonds, or currencies, such as the yen or euro, as these investments may not be affected by a drop in the price of the US dollar. Additionally, investors could consider other investments, such as real estate, commodities, or precious metals, as these investments may provide a hedge against a potential decline in the value of the US dollar. By diversifying their investments, investors can spread their risk across different asset classes, which can help to minimize the impact of any single event, such as a US dollar crash, on their overall portfolio. Furthermore, diversification can also help to improve the risk-adjusted returns of a portfolio by reducing the overall volatility of the portfolio.

Investing in alternative assets such as gold, real estate, or foreign currencies can be a valuable strategy to minimize the risks associated with a potential US dollar crash. These assets can provide a hedge against inflation and a decline in the value of the US dollar. For example, gold is a popular choice for investors as it has historically retained its value during times of economic uncertainty and market volatility. Real estate is another alternative asset that can provide a hedge against inflation as property values tend to go up in value over time.. Investing in alternative assets can also provide diversification benefits to a portfolio, which can help to spread risk and reduce overall volatility. However, investing in alternative assets does come with its own set of risks, and investors should carefully evaluate the risks and potential rewards associated with each asset class before investing.

Implementing a hedging strategy can be an effective way to protect investments against the risks associated with a potential US dollar crash. A hedging strategy involves taking a position in a financial instrument that is designed to offset possible losses in another position. For example, investors can use currency hedging strategies, such as forward contracts or currency options, to protect their investments denominated in foreign currencies against the potential decline in the US dollar. In addition, investors can use options, futures, or other derivative instruments to hedge against potential losses in stock or bond positions. The effectiveness of a hedging strategy depends on the type of investment and the specific market conditions. Hedging strategies can be complex, and investors should be careful when considering the costs and risks associated with each strategy before investing in it. However, when done correctly, a hedging strategy can be an effective tool for managing risk and protecting investments against the impact of a US dollar crash.

Chapter 5

Crypto

The sudden rise and emergence of cryptocurrencies and blockchain technology has introduced a new level of disruption to the traditional global currency market. Cryptocurrencies such as Bitcoin, Ethereum, and Litecoin are decentralized digital currencies that operate independently of traditional banking systems. Transactions are processed on a distributed ledger called a blockchain, which provides a high level of security and transparency.

The potential benefits of using cryptocurrencies as an alternative to traditional currencies include faster transaction processing times, lower transaction fees, and increased privacy. On top of that, cryptocurrencies may provide a way for individuals and businesses to avoid the risks associated with currency fluctuations and government policies that can impact traditional currencies.

But really, there are also potential risks associated with the use of cryptocurrencies, including the potential for increased volatility and the risk of fraud or hacking. On top of that, the lack of regulation and oversight in the cryptocurrency market has raised concerns about potential financial instability.

At the same time, the continued growth and development of cryptocurrencies and blockchain technology suggests that they will continue to play an important role in the global currency market. Governments and financial institutions they are increasingly exploring the potential benefits and risks of using cryptocurrencies, and it remains to be seen how the market will evolve in the coming years.

Stablecoins are a type of cryptocurrency that are designed to be less volatile than other cryptocurrencies, such as Bitcoin. They are typically backed by a reserve of traditional currencies or assets, such as the US dollar or gold, which helps to stabilize their value. Some stablecoins are also designed to be pegged to a specific currency, such as the US dollar or the euro.

One potential benefit of stablecoins is that they could provide a more stable and reliable medium of exchange than other cryptocurrencies. This could make them more appealing to businesses and individuals who are looking for an alternative to traditional currencies but are hesitant to invest in more volatile cryptocurrencies.

To be real, there are also potential risks associated with stablecoins. For example, there may be concerns about the stability of the reserve assets that back the stablecoin, particularly if those assets are not held in a transparent and secure manner. Additionally, there may be concerns about the potential for regulatory challenges and oversight, particularly if stablecoins become more widely adopted as a means of payment.

Blockchain technology has the potential to revolutionize cross-border payments by providing a faster, cheaper, and more secure means of conducting transactions. Because blockchain transactions are processed on a decentralized ledger, they can be completed without the need for intermediaries. This reduces the time and cost associated with cross-border payments, that increases transparency and security.

One of the key benefits of using blockchain technology for cross-border payments is that it can eliminate the need for foreign exchange conversions. Cryptocurrencies, which are often used in blockchain-based transactions, are not subject to the same currency exchange fees and rates as traditional currencies. This can save businesses and individuals a significant amount of money when conducting international transactions.

In addition to reducing costs, blockchain-based cross-border payments can also increase the speed and efficiency of transactions. Because blockchain transactions are processed in near-real-time, they can be completed much faster than traditional cross-border transactions, which can take several days or even weeks to complete.

But hold up, there are also potential risks associated with blockchain-based cross-border payments. Kind of like, the lack of regulation and oversight in the cryptocurrency market can make it difficult to ensure the security and legitimacy of transactions. At the same time the volatility of cryptocurrencies can pose a risk to individuals and businesses that rely on stable currency values for financial stability.

At the same time, the potential benefits of blockchain-based cross-border payments are significant, and the technology is likely to continue to gain traction as more individuals and businesses seek to reduce the time, cost, and complexity of international transactions.

The potential applications of smart contracts are vast, ranging from financial transactions to legal contracts and even supply chain management. One of the key benefits of smart contracts is their ability to automate complex business processes, which can lead to increased efficiency and cost savings.

Smart contracts work by using a set of pre-defined rules and conditions to automatically execute transactions when certain criteria are met. For example, a smart contract could be programmed to release payment to a supplier once a shipment of goods has been received and verified. This automation eliminates the need for intermediaries such as banks or lawyers, which can reduce the cost and complexity of executing transactions.

Another benefit of smart contracts is their transparency and immutability. Because smart contracts are executed on a blockchain ledger, they are transparent and accessible to all parties involved in the transaction. This can help to reduce the risk of fraud or disputes by providing a clear and auditable record of all transactions.

In addition to their efficiency and transparency, smart contracts also have the potential to disrupt traditional legal and financial systems by providing a more secure and reliable means of executing transactions. By eliminating intermediaries and relying on code rather than human discretion, smart contracts can reduce the risk of errors, fraud, and other types of malfeasance.

Despite their potential benefits, there are also potential risks associated with smart contracts. For example, if the code underlying a smart contract is flawed or contains errors, it could lead to unintended consequences or even financial losses. Additionally, the lack of regulation and oversight in the smart contract space can make it difficult to ensure the security and reliability of these contracts.

Overall, the potential of smart contracts to disrupt traditional legal and financial systems is significant, and this technology is likely to play an increasingly important role in the future of business and commerce.

Central Bank Digital Currencies, or CBDCs, are digital versions of fiat currencies that are issued and backed by a country's central bank. Unlike cryptocurrencies, CBDCs are not decentralized and are under the control of the issuing central bank. CBDCs are intended to provide a digital alternative to physical cash, allowing for faster, cheaper, and more secure transactions. They can also potentially provide a new tool for central banks to implement monetary policy and address issues such as financial inclusion and payment system efficiency. CBDCs are currently being explored by many central banks around the world, with some countries, such as China, already having launched pilot programs. However, the implementation of CBDCs poses several challenges, such as ensuring security and privacy, mitigating risks such as money laundering and cyber-attacks, and balancing innovation with financial stability. The introduction of CBDCs could also potentially have significant implications for the traditional banking system and the wider financial ecosystem.

The rise of cryptocurrencies and blockchain technology has the potential to disrupt the traditional global currency market in several ways. Cryptocurrencies provide an alternative to traditional currencies, offering faster and cheaper cross-border transactions, increased privacy and security, and the potential for decentralization and disintermediation. Blockchain technology, the underlying technology behind many cryptocurrencies, offers a decentralized and transparent ledger system that can reduce the time, cost, and complexity of cross-border payments. Central bank digital currencies (CBDCs) could potentially further disrupt the traditional currency market by providing a government-backed digital currency that could compete with traditional currencies and cryptocurrencies. While there are potential benefits and risks associated with the disruption of the global currency market by crypto and blockchain technology, the potential for increased efficiency and innovation is clear.

Chapter 6

Central Banks and the Currency Market

The US dollar holds a prominent position as the global reserve currency, playing a vital role in international trade and finance. Its status as a reserve currency grants it widespread acceptance and use for transactions worldwide. As a result, the US dollar's performance and stability have significant implications for global economic stability. This introductory section aims to provide an overview of the US dollar as a global reserve currency, highlighting its historical significance and the factors that have contributed to its dominance. Understanding the US dollar's role as a reserve currency sets the stage for exploring the potential impact of central banks in currency markets, particularly in the context of a US dollar crash. By examining the dynamics of the US dollar as a global reserve currency, we can gain insights into the potential consequences and actions of central banks in safeguarding the stability of currency markets.

Central banks play a critical role in currency markets, influencing the supply, demand, and value of currencies through various monetary policy tools. Their actions and decisions can have a profound impact on the stability and functioning of currency markets, including the US dollar. Central banks are responsible for maintaining price stability, promoting economic growth, and safeguarding the financial system within their respective countries. Through measures such as interest rate adjustments, open market operations, and currency interventions, central banks can directly influence exchange rates and indirectly shape the value of the US dollar in global currency markets. Understanding the significance of central banks in currency markets is essential to comprehend their potential role in mitigating or exacerbating the effects of a US dollar crash. In the following parts of this chapter, we will delve deeper into the actions and policies of central banks and explore their potential responses in the event of a US dollar crisis.

The potential role of central banks in a US dollar crash is a subject of significant interest and speculation among economists, policymakers, and financial market participants. As guardians of monetary policy and overseers of financial stability, central banks have a crucial role to play in navigating currency crises. The US dollar, being a global reserve currency, holds a unique position in international trade and finance. Any significant disruptions to its value and stability can have far-reaching implications for global markets. Central banks, through their policies and interventions, have the potential to either mitigate or amplify the impact of a US dollar crash. In this chapter, we will explore the potential actions and strategies that central banks may employ to manage and mitigate the risks associated with a US dollar crisis, examining the tools at their disposal and the potential consequences for the global economy.

The historical role of central banks in currency markets is characterized by their interventions aimed at maintaining stability and managing currency fluctuations. Central banks have a long-standing tradition of utilizing various tools and strategies to influence their domestic currencies and navigate turbulent currency markets. These interventions can take different forms, including direct interventions through buying or selling currencies, implementing monetary policy measures, and setting interest rates. Throughout history, central banks have intervened during times of currency crises or excessive volatility to stabilize exchange rates and protect their economies from adverse effects. Examples of such interventions include massive foreign exchange market interventions by central banks to defend their currencies, coordinated efforts among central banks to stabilize currency values, and the establishment of currency swap lines to provide liquidity during periods of market stress. By delving into the historical interventions of central banks in currency markets, we can gain valuable insights into their potential role in managing and mitigating the risks associated with a US dollar crash.

Central banks around the world have implemented various actions to stabilize or manipulate exchange rates in order to safeguard their economies and maintain a competitive edge in the global market. One prominent example is the intervention by the Bank of Japan, which has frequently intervened in the foreign exchange market to prevent excessive appreciation of the yen. This intervention has involved massive purchases of foreign currencies, particularly during periods when the yen's strength threatened Japan's export competitiveness. Similarly, the Swiss National Bank has intervened to prevent the excessive appreciation of the Swiss franc, as a stronger currency could negatively impact the country's export-oriented economy. The Swiss National Bank has engaged in large-scale purchases of foreign currencies and utilized negative interest rates to deter capital inflows. These examples demonstrate how central banks employ interventions to stabilize exchange rates and shield their economies from adverse effects caused by abrupt currency movements. The actions taken by central banks highlight their crucial role in managing exchange rate fluctuations and fostering economic stability.

Central banks have a range of tools and mechanisms at their disposal when conducting currency interventions. One common tool is direct market intervention, where central banks buy or sell currencies in the foreign exchange market to influence exchange rates. This can be done through open market operations or through the use of foreign exchange reserves. Additionally, central banks can adjust interest rates to impact currency values. By increasing interest rates, central banks can attract foreign investment and strengthen their currency. Conversely, lowering interest rates can encourage domestic borrowing and spending, potentially weakening the currency. Central banks also utilize forward guidance, which involves providing public statements and guidance on future monetary policy actions. Such guidance can influence market expectations and impact currency valuations. Lastly, central banks may implement capital controls, which are measures to restrict the flow of capital in and out of a country. These controls can help stabilize exchange rates and prevent speculative activities. The utilization of these tools and mechanisms reflects the ability of central banks to actively manage and intervene in currency markets to achieve desired outcomes.

Central banks closely monitor economic indicators such as inflation, economic growth, employment rates, and trade imbalances. These factors play a crucial role in shaping their decisions regarding currency market interventions. For instance, if a country's exports are struggling due to an overvalued currency, the central bank may intervene to weaken the currency and enhance export competitiveness. Conversely, if inflationary pressures are rising, the central bank may intervene to strengthen the currency and curb inflationary effects.

Political and geopolitical events can significantly impact currency markets. Central banks consider factors such as changes in government policies, trade disputes, geopolitical tensions, and international relations when determining their interventions. For example, political instability or conflicts may prompt central banks to take actions to stabilize their currency in the face of uncertainty or to mitigate potential economic shocks.

Each central bank operates under specific mandates and policies, which guide their actions in currency markets. These mandates often prioritize goals such as maintaining price stability, promoting full employment, and ensuring financial stability. The central bank's policies and guidelines play a significant role in determining the extent and nature of their interventions. Additionally, central banks may have specific exchange rate regimes, such as fixed or floating exchange rates, which shape their approach to currency market interventions.

A US dollar crash refers to a significant and sudden decline in the value of the US dollar against other major currencies. Various scenarios can contribute to such an event, including mounting government debt, trade imbalances, economic downturns, or geopolitical tensions. These factors can erode investor confidence in the US dollar, leading to a rapid sell-off and depreciation.

In the event of a US dollar crash, central banks around the world would closely monitor the situation and respond accordingly. They may take measures to stabilize their domestic currencies, such as selling their US dollar reserves, implementing capital controls, or adjusting interest rates. Central banks may also collaborate to coordinate international efforts to restore stability and prevent further currency volatility.

Central bank interventions can have a significant impact on the stability of the US dollar during a potential crash. Their actions can influence currency exchange rates, market sentiment, and investor confidence. By implementing appropriate monetary policies and interventions, central banks can mitigate the severity of a US dollar crash and restore stability to the global currency markets.

Central banks play a critical role in shaping the value of the US dollar through their monetary policy decisions. Factors such as interest rates, money supply, and inflation targets can significantly influence the exchange rate and the overall strength of the US dollar.

In times of economic crises or to stimulate economic growth, central banks may resort to unconventional monetary policies. These policies, such as quantitative easing or negative interest rates, can have substantial implications for the US dollar. By injecting liquidity into the financial system or altering interest rate differentials, central banks can impact currency values, capital flows, and investor perceptions.

Central banks' communication strategies and public statements can significantly impact currency markets, including the US dollar. The tone, clarity, and consistency of central bank messages can shape market expectations, influence investor sentiment, and impact exchange rates.

The stability and integrity of currency markets are crucial for global economic stability. This section provides an overview of international initiatives and frameworks aimed at regulating currency markets. Organizations like the International Monetary Fund (IMF) and the Financial Stability Board (FSB) play a significant role in coordinating efforts to enhance transparency, monitor market activities, and promote responsible behavior in currency trading.

Central banks often play a vital role in shaping and implementing currency market regulations within their respective jurisdictions. They contribute to the design and enforcement of rules and standards that govern currency trading activities, market infrastructure, and financial institutions' conduct

In light of the potential risks associated with a US dollar crash, policymakers and market participants have considered various reforms to mitigate these risks

Chapter 7

Preparing for Currency Change

The importance of preparing for a potential transition away from the US dollar as the global reserve currency cannot be understated. As the current dominant reserve currency, the US dollar holds a central position in the global financial system. However, the shifting dynamics of the global economy, emerging economic powers, and technological advancements are challenging the status quo. Being prepared for a potential transition is essential to navigate the potential disruptions and seize opportunities that may arise.

The transition away from the US dollar as the global reserve currency presents both challenges and opportunities. On one hand, it involves significant economic, financial, and geopolitical complexities. The adjustment process could impact international trade, investment flows, and monetary policies worldwide. On the other hand, it opens doors to innovation, diversification, and the development of new financial instruments and systems.

The purpose of this chapter is to provide insights and practical guidance for individuals, businesses, and governments in preparing for a potential transition away from the US dollar as the global reserve currency. By examining the importance of this transition, discussing the challenges and opportunities involved, and offering practical advice, this chapter aims to empower readers to make informed decisions and take proactive steps to adapt to the changing global economic landscape. Whether it is diversifying currency holdings, exploring alternative investment strategies, or participating in discussions on international monetary reforms, this chapter will equip readers with the knowledge and tools needed to prepare for a potential currency transition

Examination of the factors driving the need for a potential transition away from the US dollar reveals a shifting global economic landscape that calls for a reevaluation of the dominant reserve currency. Several factors contribute to this need. Firstly, the rise of emerging economies, such as China and India, has led to an increasing share of global economic output and trade conducted in their respective currencies. This shift challenges the historical dominance of the US dollar and prompts a reassessment of the currency composition in international transactions.

Furthermore, changing trade patterns and economic alliances play a significant role in driving the need for transition. The formation of regional trade blocs, such as the European Union and the Comprehensive and Progressive Agreement for Trans-Pacific Partnership (CPTPP), encourages countries within these blocs to conduct more trade in their regional currencies. As regional economic integration deepens, the importance of a single global reserve currency diminishes, creating the impetus for exploring alternative currencies.

Moreover, technological advancements, particularly in the realm of digital currencies and blockchain technology, have opened new possibilities for cross-border transactions.

Cryptocurrencies and central bank digital currencies (CBDCs) have the potential to streamline and decentralize international transactions, reducing reliance on traditional currencies. As these technological innovations continue to develop, they present opportunities for a more diverse and inclusive international monetary system.

Overall, the need for a potential transition away from the US dollar as the global reserve currency is driven by the rise of emerging economies, changing trade patterns, and technological advancements.

While the US dollar has served as the dominant reserve currency for decades, it is not without its shortcomings.

One limitation is the potential for overreliance on a single currency. The concentration of global reserves in the US dollar creates vulnerabilities, as any disruptions or instability in the US economy can have far-reaching consequences for the entire international monetary system. This interdependence can amplify systemic risks and contribute to financial instability.

Additionally, the current system is subject to the policies and decisions of the issuing country, in this case, the United States. Changes in monetary policy, fiscal decisions, or political developments can have significant impacts on the global economy and financial markets. This dependency on a single sovereign nation raises questions about the equitable distribution of economic power and decision-making authority.

Furthermore, the global reserve currency system may perpetuate economic imbalances and inequalities. Countries that rely heavily on the US dollar for international transactions face exchange rate risks and potential fluctuations in the value of their own currencies. This can lead to challenges in managing their economies, particularly for developing nations.

Moreover, the dominance of the US dollar can create challenges for countries seeking to diversify their currency reserves or reduce their exposure to US dollar-related risks. Financial and trade dependencies on a single currency can limit policy flexibility and hinder economic autonomy.

Considering these limitations and vulnerabilities, it becomes increasingly important to explore alternative reserve currency arrangements and diversify the global monetary system to enhance stability, resilience, and inclusiveness.

THE DOLLARS DEMISE

52